Activity Book 2

Helen Casey

Contents

Unit		Page
S	Welcome to Rooftops School	2
1	At Grandma's house	6
2	At school	15
R	Rooftops Review 1	24
3	In the countryside	26
4	At the station	35
R	Rooftops Review 2	44
5	At the farm	46
6	At the fair	55
R	Rooftops Review 3	64
	Halloween	66
	Christmas	67
	Easter	68
	Culture mini-books	69

Lesson 1 Vocabulary

 # Welcome to Rooftops School

1 Read and colour. Count and write.

 pens 15   rubbers ___   crayons ___

 pencils ___    bags ___    books ___

Lesson 2 Vocabulary

1 **Count and write.**

~~pencil cases~~   desks   rulers   pencils   chairs

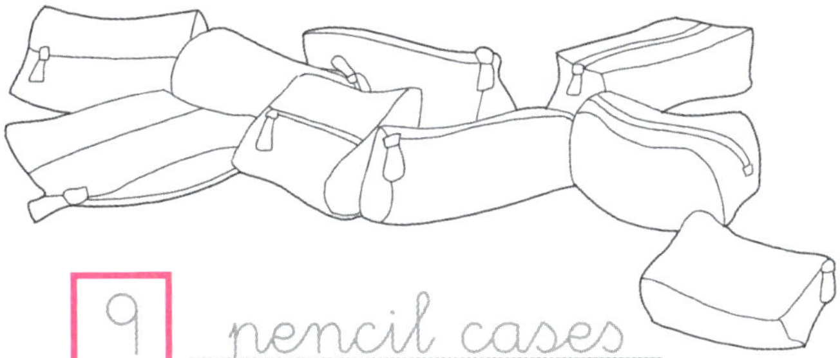

9	pencil cases
☐	_____
☐	_____
☐	_____
☐	_____

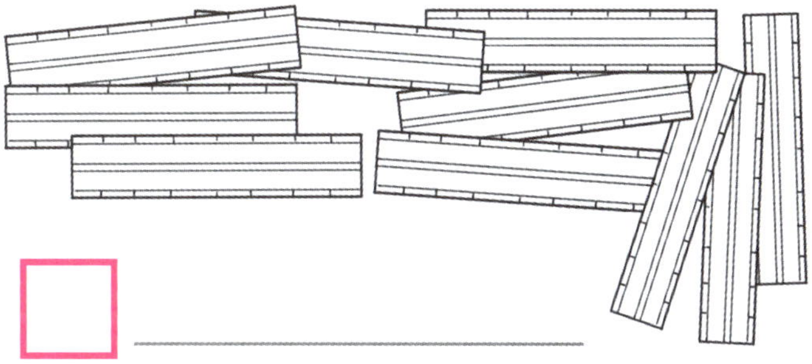

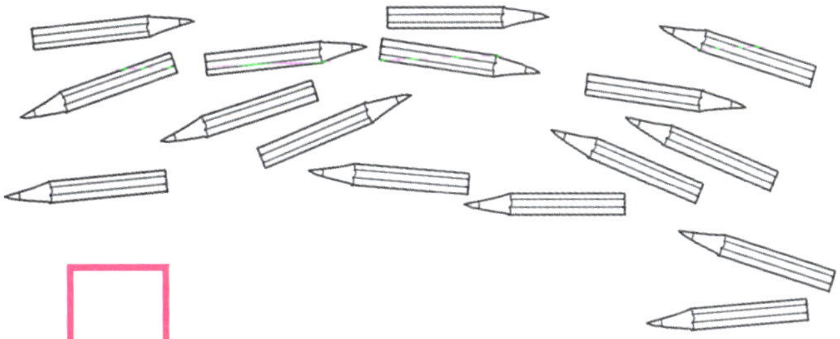

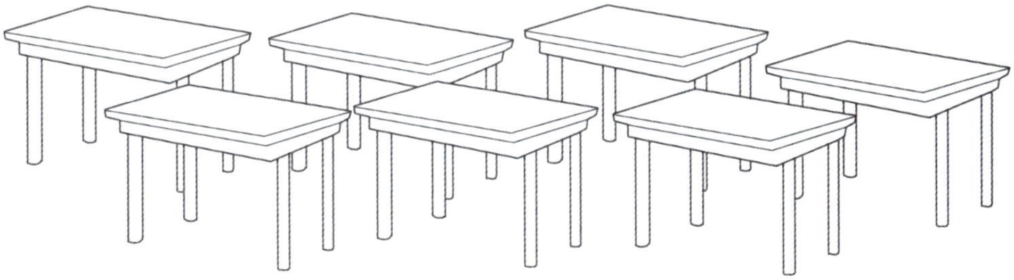

2 **What's in your bag? Count and write. Draw.**

___ pencil case(s)

___ ruler(s)

___ book(s)

___ pen(s)

___ pencil(s)

___ rubber(s)

___ jumper(s)

Lesson 3 Vocabulary

1 Look and write.

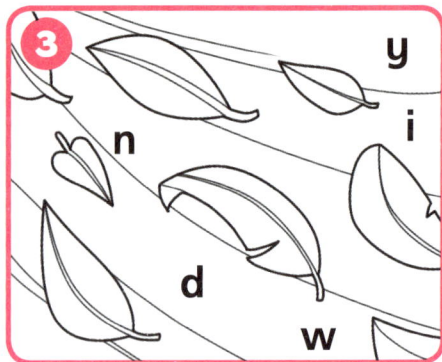

It's _____.   It's _____.   It's _____.

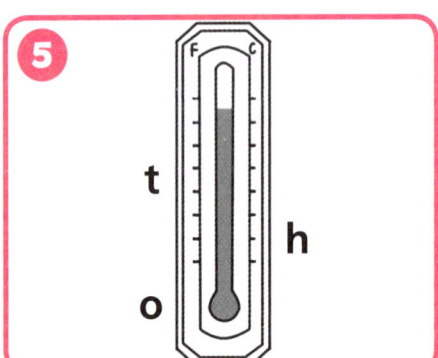
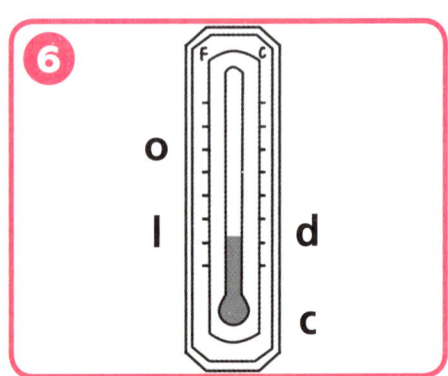

It's _____.   It's _____.   It's _____.

2 Be creative — Draw the weather today. Write.

It's _____.

Lesson 4 Vocabulary

1 Look and write.

spring   summer   autumn   winter

_____

_____

_____

_____

2 Remember and write.

School words	Weather	Seasons
_____	_____	_____
_____	_____	_____
_____	_____	_____
_____	_____	_____
_____	_____	

Lesson 1 Vocabulary

At Grandma's house

1 Look and write.

> living room   dining room   kitchen   ~~bathroom~~
> bedroom   garage   garden   hall

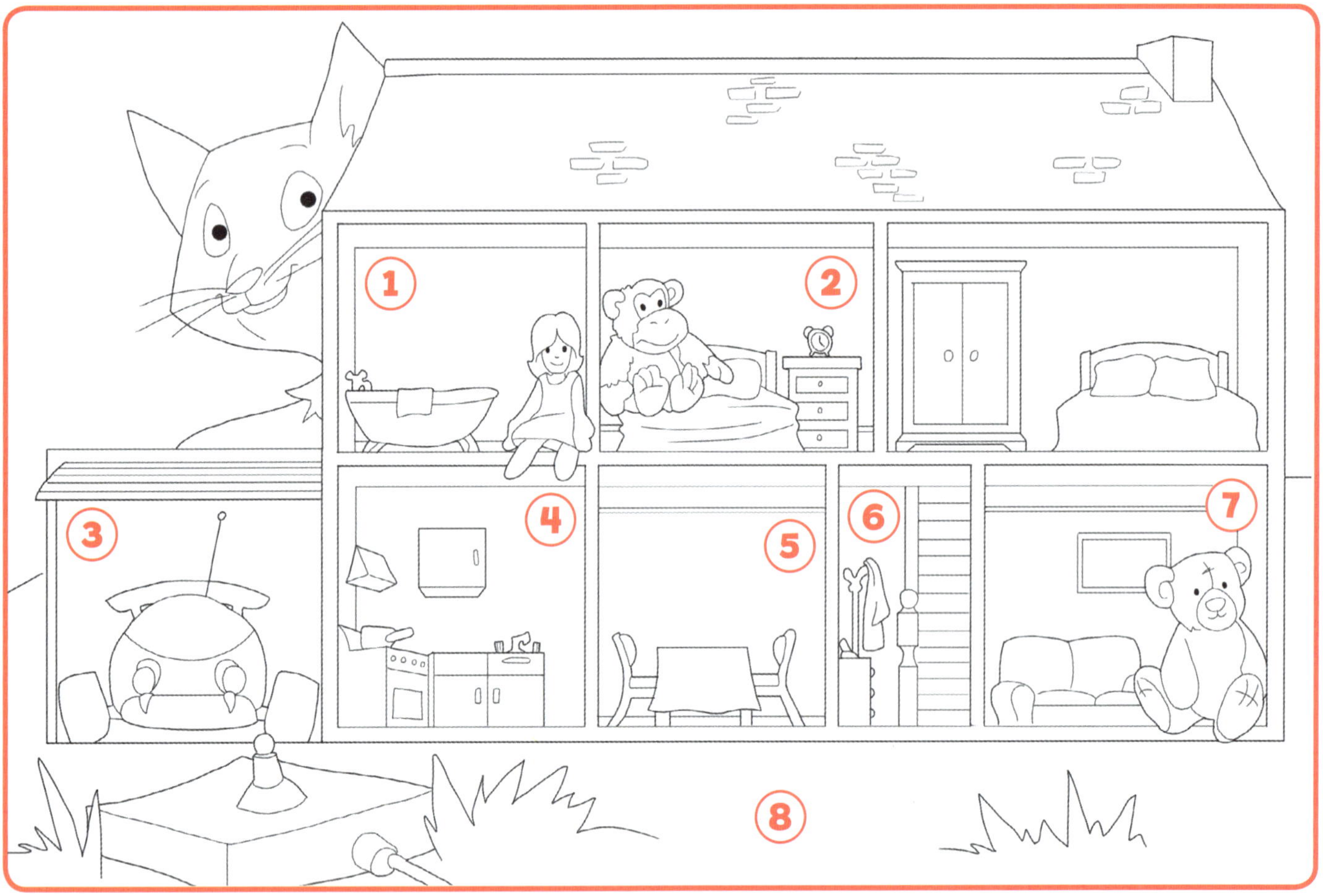

1 bathroom
2 _____
3 _____
4 _____
5 _____
6 _____
7 _____
8 _____

Finished?
Find and colour: doll, teddy, car, cat.

Lesson 2 Grammar

1 **Look, read and match.**

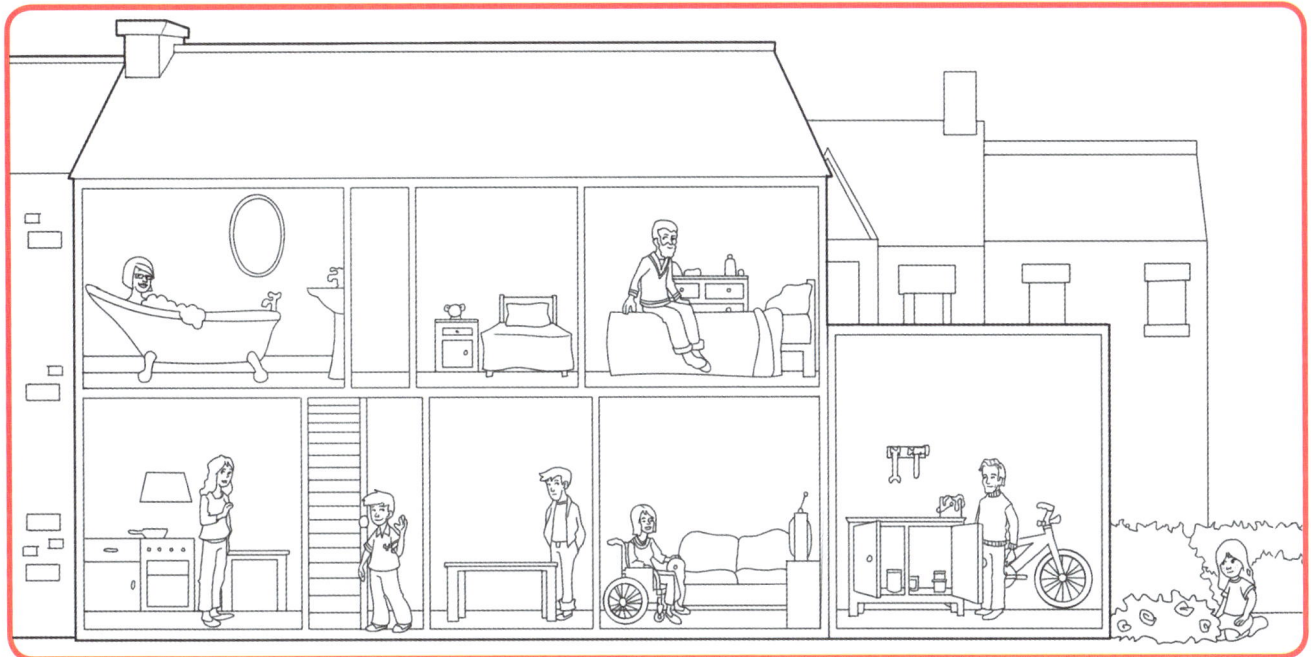

Where's …?

He's in the hall.

She's in the bathroom.

He's in the garage.

She's in the living room.

2 **Look again and write.**

kitchen   ~~garden~~   bedroom   dining room

1 Where's Anna?   She's in the _garden_.

2 Where's Mum?   She's _____ _____ _____.

3 _____ Dad?   He's _____ _____ _____.

4 _____ Grandpa?   _____

Finished?
Draw a cat in the picture. Write a question and answer.

7

Lesson 3 Culture

1 Listen, guess and number. 🔊 20

kitchen   living room
garden   bathroom

2 Look and write.

He's in the _____.

She's in the _____.

She's in the _____.

He's in the _____.

3 Be creative   Draw your home. Label the rooms.

Lesson 4 Everyday language and Values

1 💭 Think   Circle the children helping at home.

2 Write. Look and tick ✔.

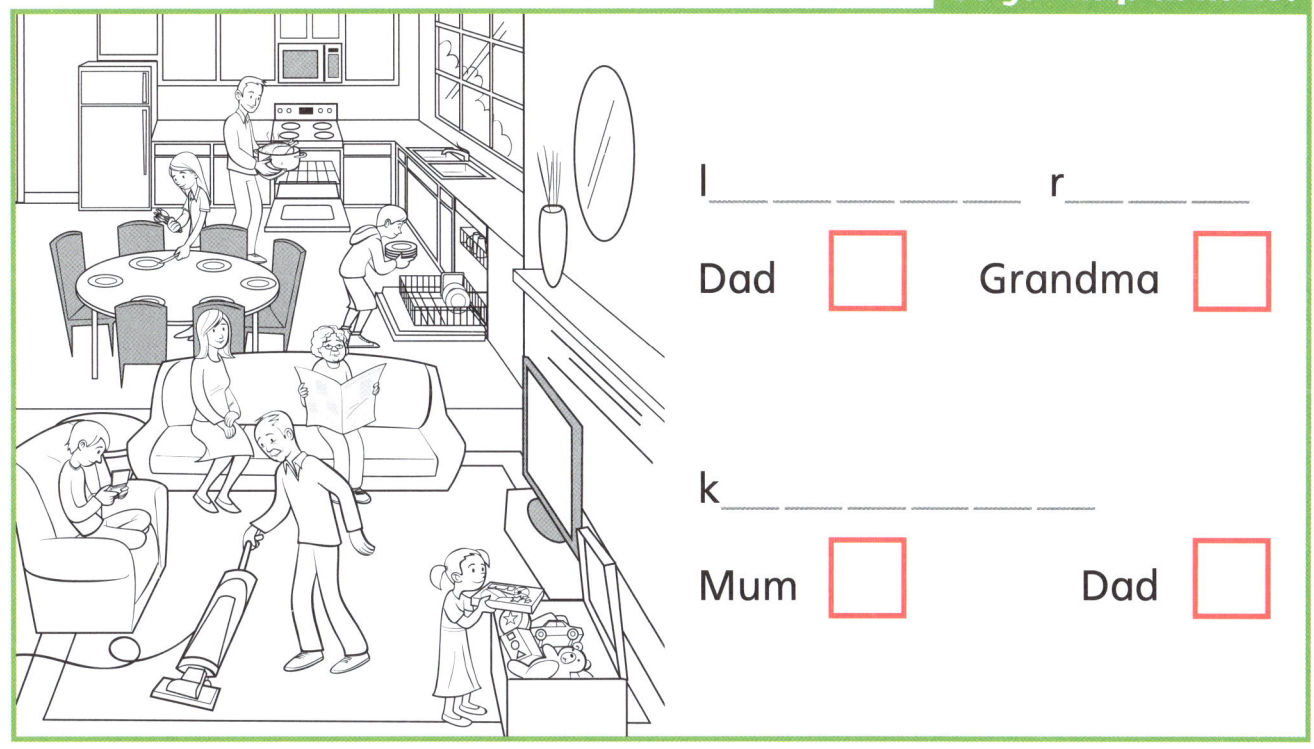

l_____   r_____

Dad ☐   Grandma ☐

k_____

Mum ☐   Dad ☐

3 💬 Communicate   Write. Tick ✔ the ones you do. Ask your family.

I can help in the _____.   I can help in my _____.   I can help in the _____.

1 Lesson 5 Story

Where's Kitty?

1 💭 **Think** Remember the story.
Number the pictures in order. Write.

| hall bathroom bedroom ~~living room~~ dining room |

 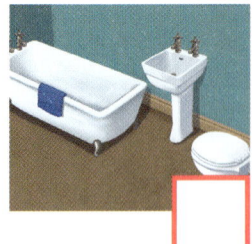   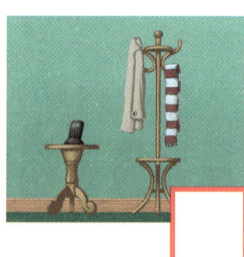

living room _____ _____ _____ _____

2 💡 **Be creative** Match. Draw Kitty and write.

①  ② ③  ④  ⑤

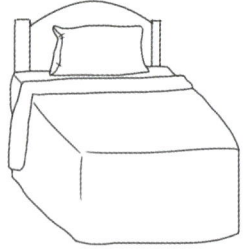 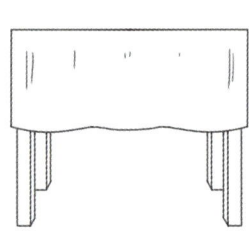   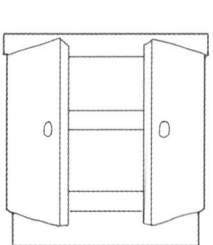

Where's Kitty? She's _____.

Finished?
Write a list of the things Anna and Oscar find in the story.

Lesson 6 Vocabulary and Grammar

1 **Look and circle.**

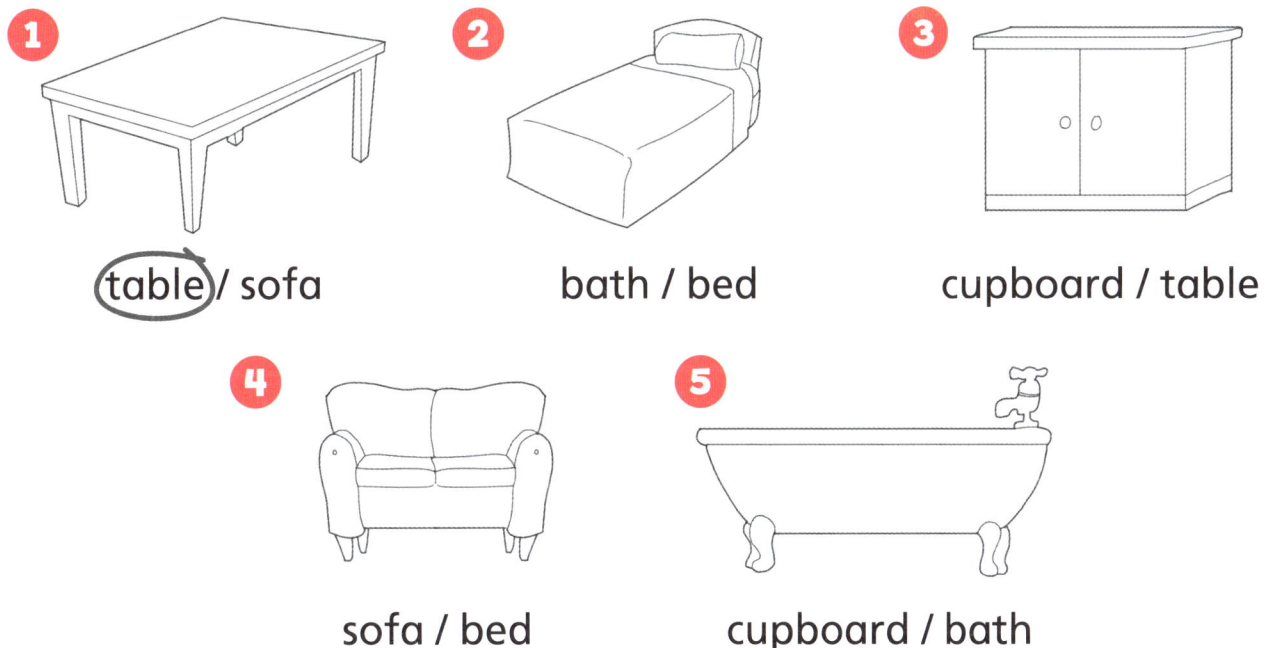

1. (table) / sofa
2. bath / bed
3. cupboard / table
4. sofa / bed
5. cupboard / bath

2 **Join the dots and draw. Write.**

on ~~in~~ under in on   sofa bed ~~bath~~ cupboard table

1. He's _in_ the _bath_.
2. She's ___ ___ ___.
3. He's ___ ___ ___.
4. She's _____.
5. He's _____.

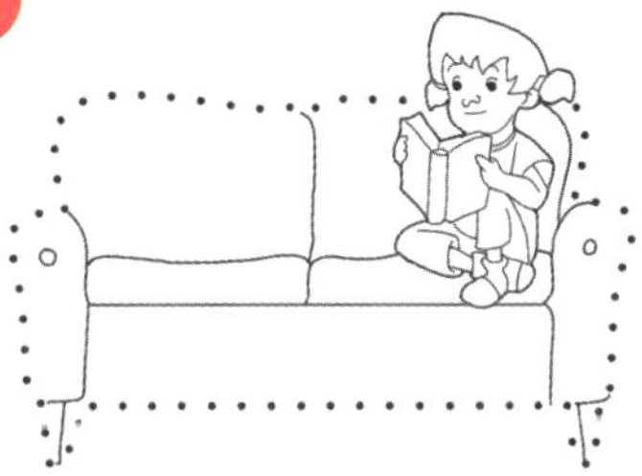

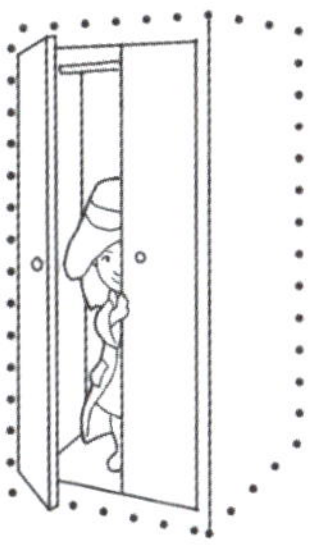

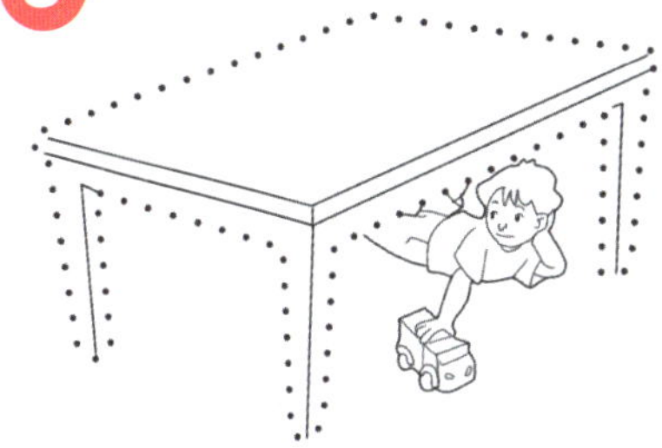

Finished?
Where can you find a bed, bath, sofa, cupboard, table? Write the rooms.

1 Lesson 7 Literacy

Rooftops Book Club

1 Find and circle. Write.

s<u>hop</u>

v_____

s_____

m_____

l_____
f_____

s_____
b_____

p	h	s	o	i	u	m	i	l	k	t	y
w	e	h	r	t	y	l	k	j	h	g	q
s	h	o	p	p	i	n	g	b	a	g	s
f	d	p	s	a	z	x	c	v	b	n	m
l	k	h	g	l	o	o	k	f	o	r	f
d	s	a	v	p	o	v	i	u	y	t	r
s	t	r	a	w	b	e	r	r	i	e	s
q	a	z	n	w	s	m	x	e	d	c	r

2 Read and write.

kitchen   in   shop   van   Where's   in

Where's Grandpa?

He's in the _____.

Where's Grandpa?

He's _____ the _____.

_____ Grandpa?

He's _____ the _____.

Book Club Extra
Where do you read? Draw. Tell your friend.

Lesson 8 Communication

1 Listen and tick ✔. Listen and chant. 🔊 31

2 💬 Communicate   Play the hide and seek game. Find Anna and win.

How to play
Take turns.
Move your counter and say.
Get to a door to
find Anna and win.

Start

You need:

It's Tommy! He's in the garden.

Pronunciation k**i**tchen / l**i**ving room

Lesson 9 Round Up

1 Look and write. Where's Anna? Find the missing room.

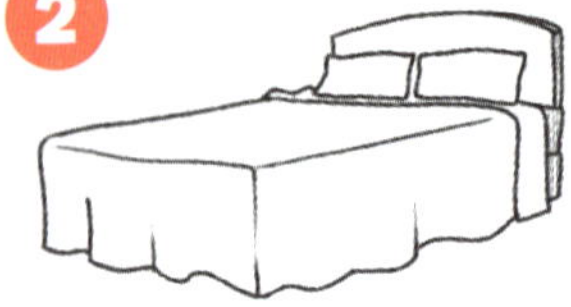

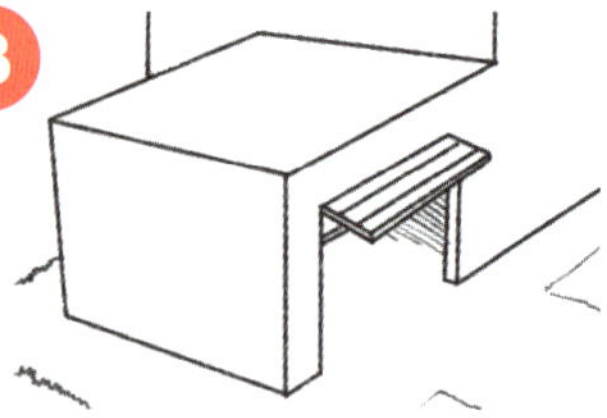

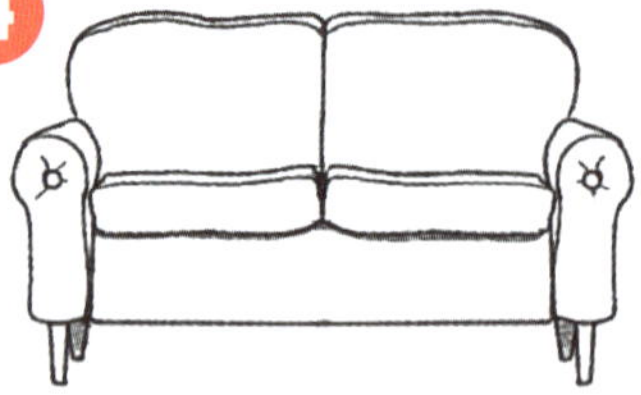

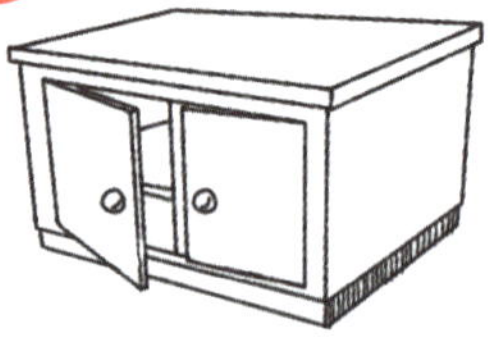

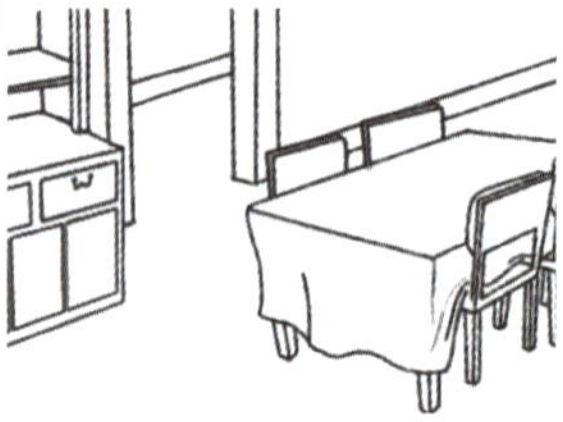

Anna is in the

8 ▢▢▢▢▢▢▢.

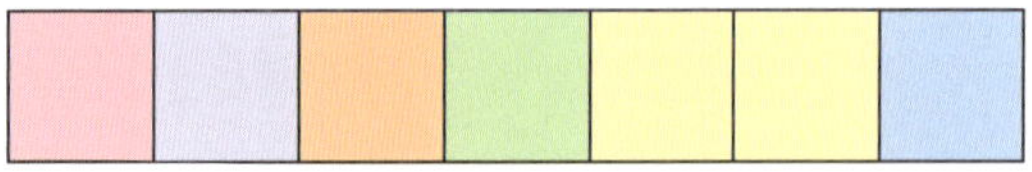

2 Read and draw. Draw and write.

Where's Anna?
She's in the living room.
She's on the sofa.
Where's Oscar?
He's _____.
He's _____.

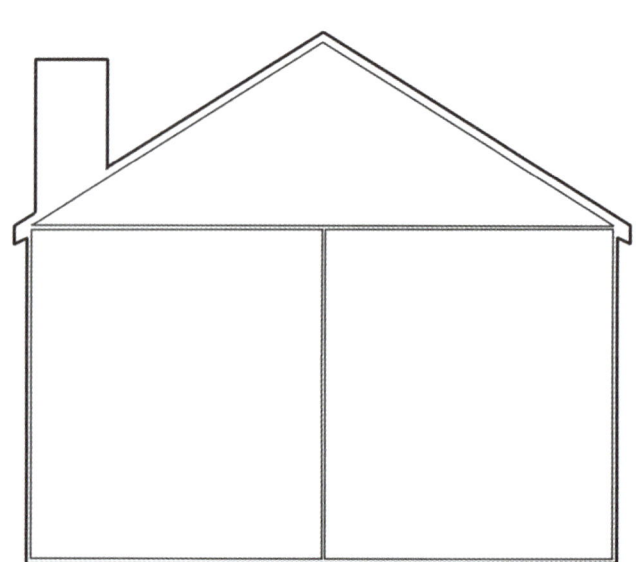

Finished?
Draw and write your favourite words in Unit 1.

Lesson 1 Vocabulary

At school

1 Read and circle. **2** Look and write.

climb catch write play football draw hop ride a bike read

1 _____ 2 _____ 3 *climb* 4 _____
5 _____ 6 _____ 7 _____ 8 _____

Finished?
Write what you can do. *I can ...*

Lesson 2 Grammar

1 Read and circle.

1 He can / (can't) ride a bike.    2 She can / can't climb.

3 She can / can't play football.   4 He can / can't read.

2 Look and write.   catch   hop   draw   write

1 He can _____.   2 She can't _____.

3 _____.   4 _____.

Finished?
Write the action words with 4 and 5 letters.

Lesson 3 Culture 2

1 Read and number.

1 This is Charlie. He's 7. He can read and draw.

2 This is Thomas. He's 8. He can play football.

3 This is Bella. She's 7. She can climb.

2 💡 Be creative **Draw yourself at school. Write.**

This is me. I'm _____.

I'm wearing _____.

I can _____.

2 Lesson 4 Everyday language and Values

1 💭 **Think** Circle the children taking turns.

2 Read and colour. Draw 1 more toy and write.

Our Values
Do you take turns?

1 a pink skipping rope
2 an orange skateboard
3 a purple scooter
4 _____

3 💬 **Communicate** Write. What do you take turns with? Look and tick ✓. Ask your family.

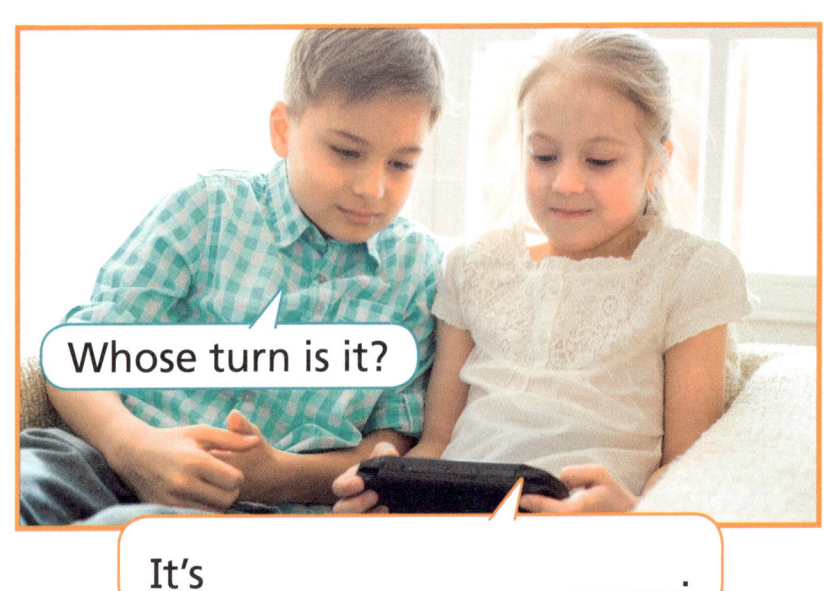

Whose turn is it?

It's _____.

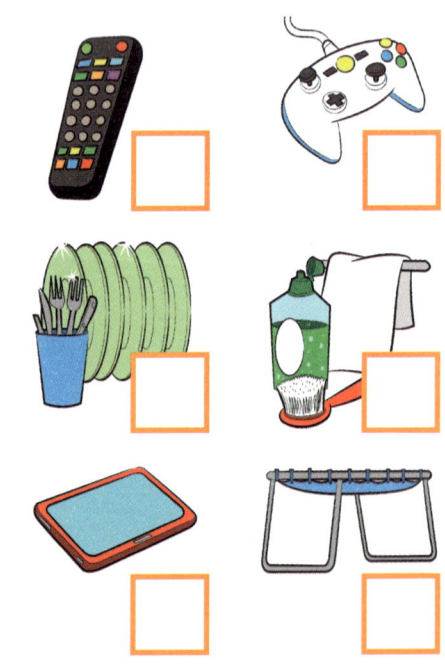

Nizzy's surprise

Lesson 5 Story 2

1 🗨 **Think** Remember the story. Number the pictures in order.

2 Where's Nizzy? Draw.

3 💡 **Be creative** When's Diwali? Tick ✓ and write.
Draw a Diwali picture.

☐ spring
☐ summer
☐ autumn
☐ winter

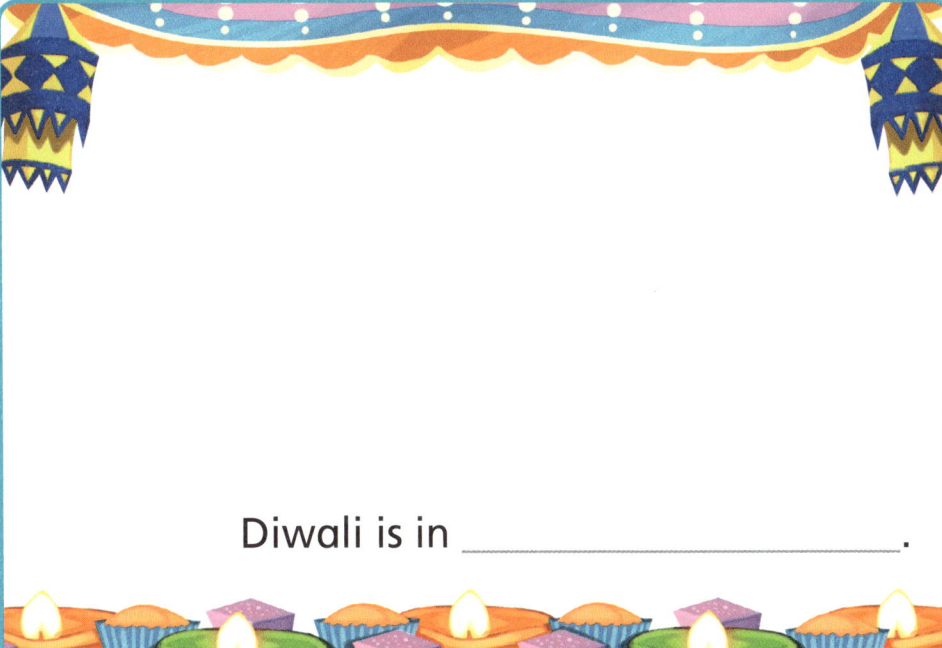

Diwali is in _____.

Finished?
Write the seasons for Christmas, Easter and Halloween.

2 Lesson 6 Vocabulary and Grammar

1 Look and write.

playground   gym   classroom
toilets   bike shed

1 _____
2 _____
3 _____
4 _____
5 _____

2 Look again and tick ✓ or cross ✗. Write.

1 gym ✓ She's in the _____gym_____.

  classroom ✗ She isn't in the _____classroom_____.

2 playground ☐ He's in the _____.

  toilets ☐ He isn't in the _____.

3 classroom ☐ She's _____.

  bike shed ☐ She isn't _____.

4 bike shed ☐ _____

  playground ☐ _____

5 toilets ☐ _____

  gym ☐ _____

Finished?
What's in your school? Write the places.

Rooftops Book Club

Lesson 7 Literacy **2**

1 Write. Complete and answer the secret question.

egg   flour   sugar   strawberries   butter

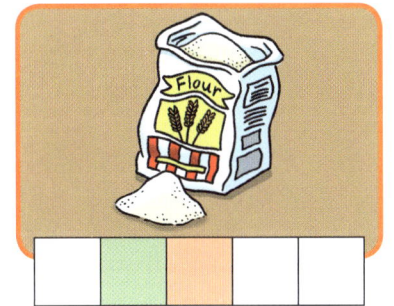

D _ y _ _ _ _ k _ c _ k _ ? _____

2 Draw and write the food.

Grandpa puts in _____,   Clunk puts in _____

_____ and _____.   and _____.

Book Club Extra
Draw a character you like. Write what he / she can do.

2 Lesson 8 Communication

1 Listen and tick ✓. Listen and chant. 🔊 52

2 💬 **Communicate** Play 3 in a row. Choose and say.

You need:

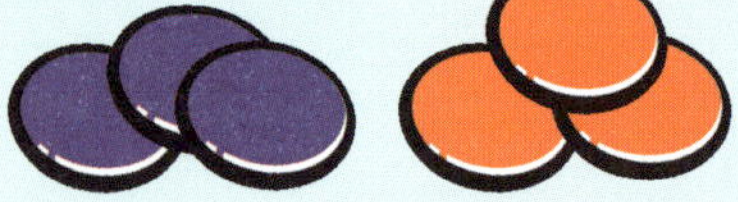

"She can't read. Red!"

22 Pronunciation skip / stop

Lesson 9 Round Up 2

1 Look and write.

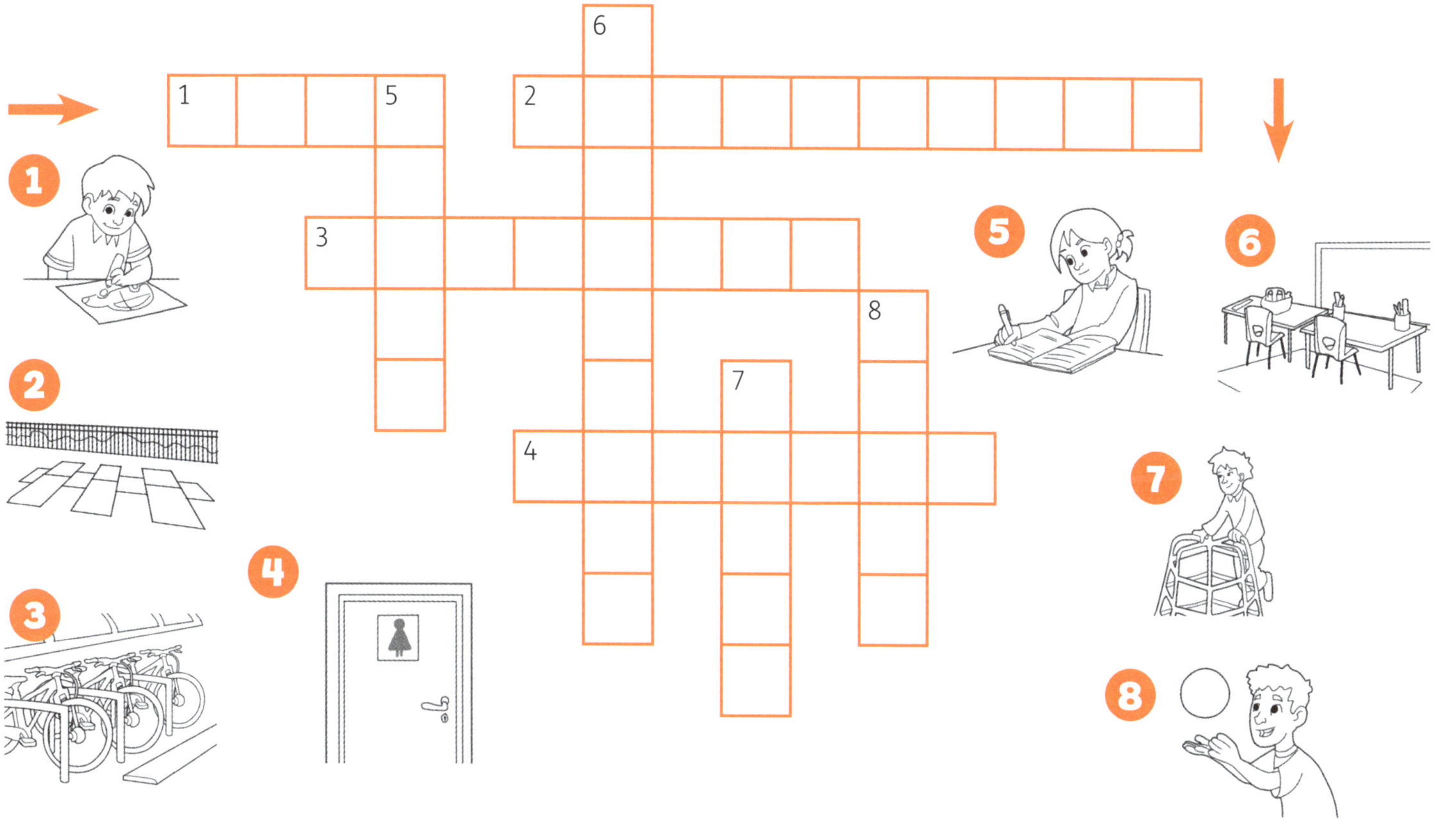

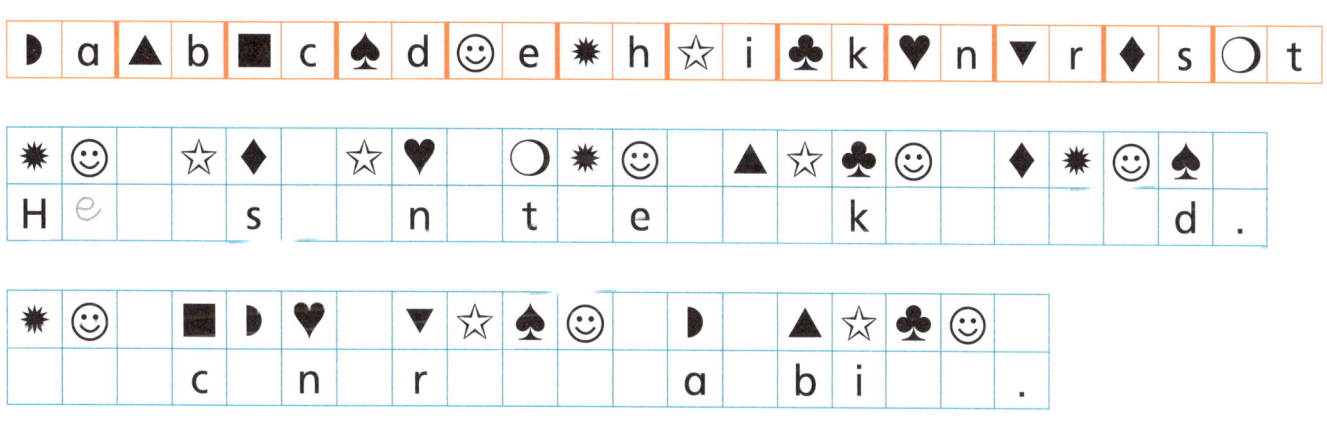

2 Complete the puzzles. Look and tick ✓.

| ◗ a | ▲ b | ■ c | ♠ d | ☺ e | ✹ h | ☆ i | ♣ k | ♥ n | ▼ r | ♦ s | ◯ t |

| ✹ | ☺ | | ☆ | ♦ | | ☆ | ♥ | | ◯ | ✹ | ☺ | | ▲ | ☆ | ♣ | ☺ | | ♦ | ✹ | ☺ | ♠ |
| H | e | | s | | | n | | | t | e | | | | k | | | | | d | . |

| ✹ | ☺ | | ■ | ◗ | ♥ | | ▼ | ☆ | ♠ | ☺ | | ◗ | | ▲ | ☆ | ♣ | ☺ |
| | | | c | | n | | r | | | | | a | | b | | i | . |

Finished?
Draw and write your favourite words in Unit 2.

23

Rooftops Review

1 💬 **Communicate**   Find and circle. Say the season and the weather.

 a yellow sofa   She can draw.   He's in the gym.

 a picnic table   He can climb.   a blue desk

 She can read.   She's in the garage.   He's in the kitchen.

Finished? Find Joey 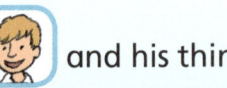 and his things   . Write the places.

Review 1

2 🗨 Think Read and write more words.

At home
bath

At school
gym

At home and school
read

3 Follow and write.

~~Where's~~   Anna   classroom   write   read   in the playground   He can   under   table

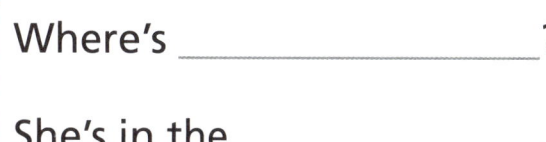

Where's _____?

She's in the _____.

She can _____.

Where's Nizzy?

He's _____.

_____ ride a bike.

Where's Anna?

She's _____ the _____.

She can _____.

Finished?
Write 4 things you take to school every day.

Lesson 1 Vocabulary

In the countryside

1 Read, number and write.

1 ~~hill~~   2 lake   3 river   4 rainbow   5 road   6 tree   7 farm   8 rock

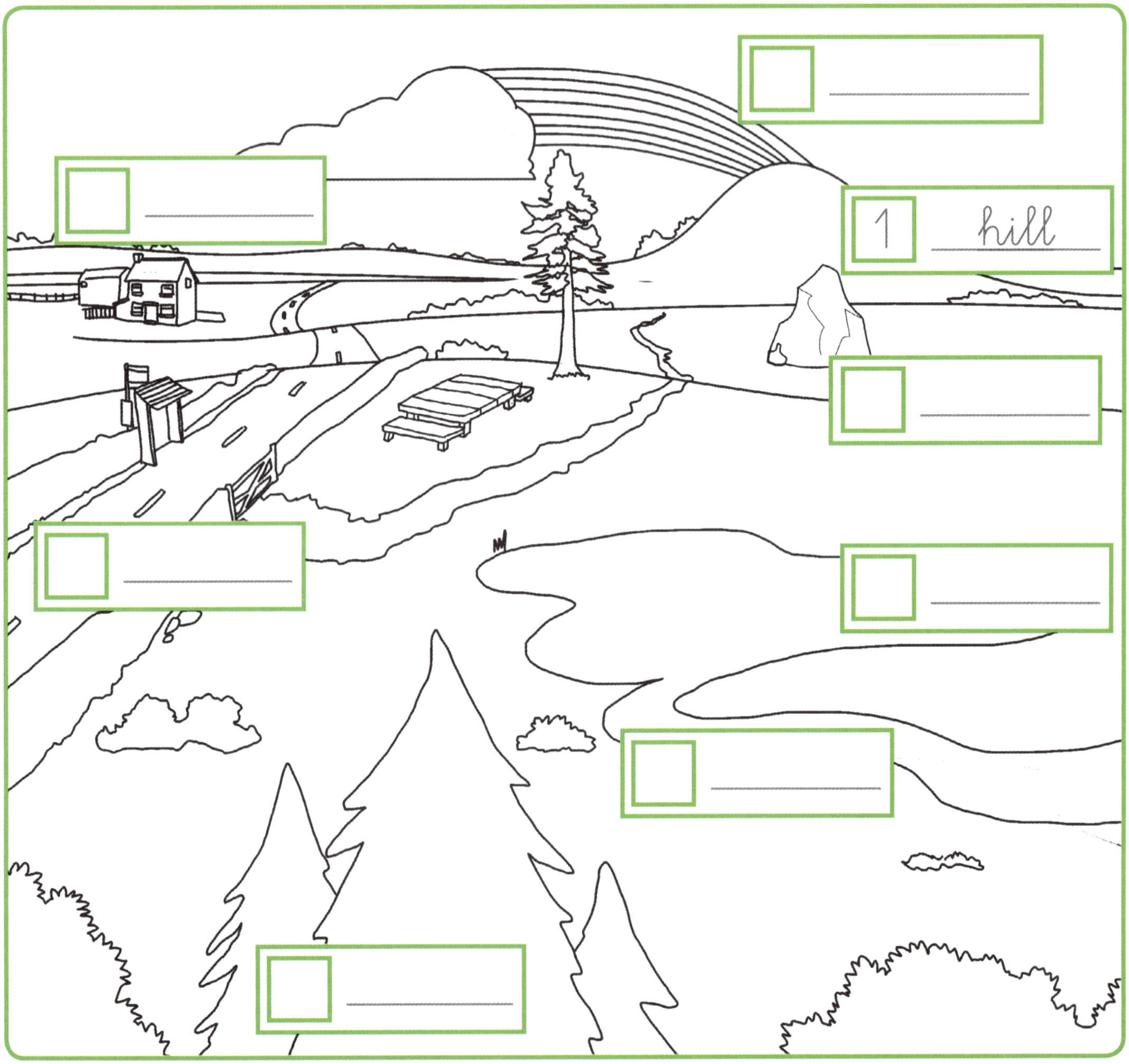

| 1 | hill |

Finished?
Write and draw three animals you can see in the countryside.

Lesson 2 Grammar **3**

1 **Circle 5 differences. Read and tick ✓.**

1 Can you see a river?   Yes, I can.   A ✓   B ☐
2 Can you see a tree?   Yes, I can.   A ☐   B ☐
3 Can you see a rock?   No, I can't.   A ☐   B ☐
4 Can you see a road?   No, I can't.   A ☐   B ☐

2 **Look and write.**

~~rock~~   farm   lake   rainbow   tree

 1 Can you see a _rock_ ? Yes, I can.

 2 Can you see a _____ ? No, I can't.

 3 _____ ?

 4 _____ ?

5 _____ ?

Finished?
Look out of the window. Write *I can see a …*

3 Lesson 3 Culture

1 Listen and number.

2 Look and write.

rock   tree   lake   road

I can see a _____. It's big.   I can see a _____. It's old.

I can see a _____. It's old.   I _____. It's big.

3 Be creative   Think of a famous place. Draw and write.

I can see a _____.

It's _____.

What a great day out!

Lesson 4 Everyday language and Values **3**

1 💬 Think Circle 5 people helping others.

2 Read and draw.

Our Values
Are you polite and helpful?

1 A boat on the river.
2 A car on the road.
3 A bike on the road.
4 A duck on the river.

3 💬 Communicate Choose and write. Act out at home.

Excuse me. Where's the _____?

park   farm
school   river

It's _____.

29

3 Lesson 5 Story — The nature reserve

1 🧠 **Think** Remember the story. Match. Write.

tree   lake   ~~tree~~   rock

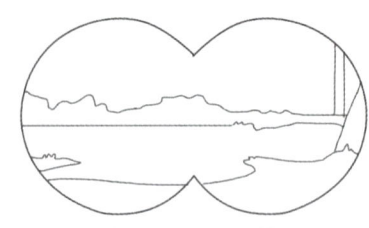

1. It's next to the _____.

2. It's behind a _tree_.

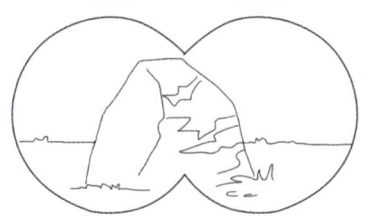

3. It's on the _____.

4. It's in front of the _____.

2 💡 **Be creative** What can Oscar see? Draw and write.

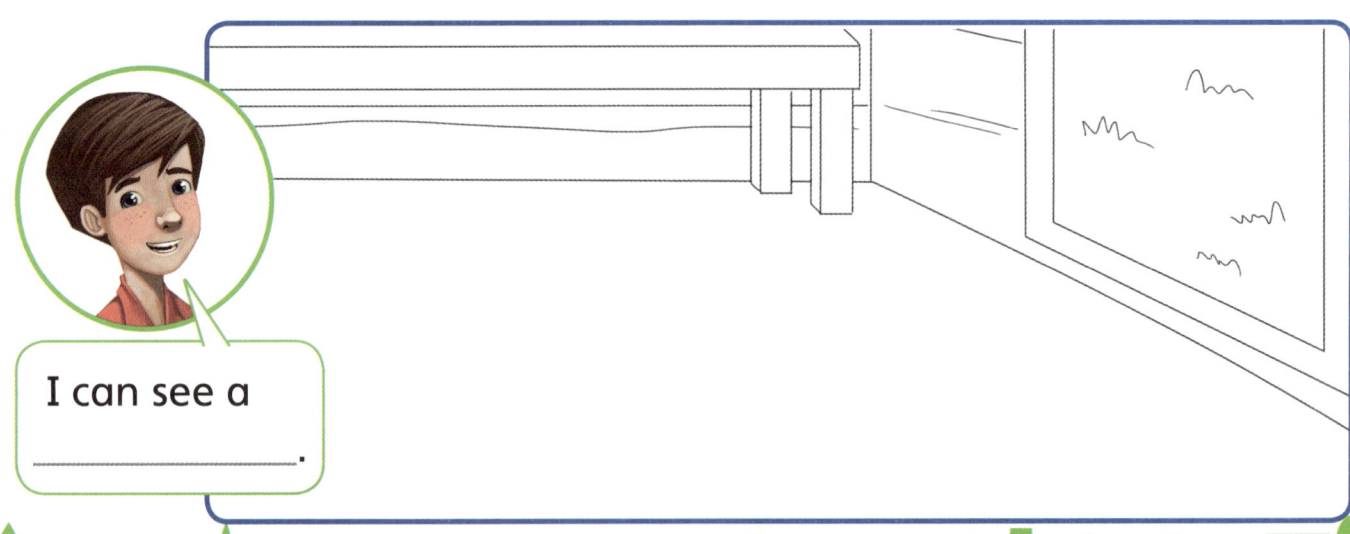

I can see a _____.

Finished? Write a list of all the animal words you know.

Lesson 6 Vocabulary and Grammar

1 Join the dots and draw. Write.

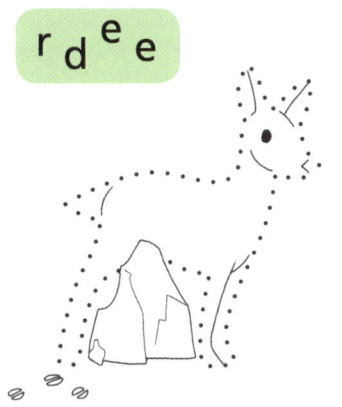

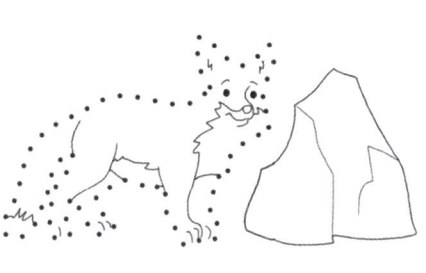

1 _deer_   2 _____   3 _____

4 _____   5 _____

2 Look again and write.

| next to   in front of   behind   in front of   next to |

 1 Where's the __deer__? It's _____ the rock.

 2 Where's the _____? It's _____.

 3 Where's the _____? It's _____ the rock.

 4 Where's the _____? _____

 5 Where's the _____? _____

Finished?
Draw an animal. Write where it is.

Lesson 7 Literacy

1 Read, follow and circle.

A big, red cake.

A small, pink cake.

A big, pink cake.

2 Read and write. Choose. Write and draw.

big   small
red   pink   black   blue
hungry   happy   sad

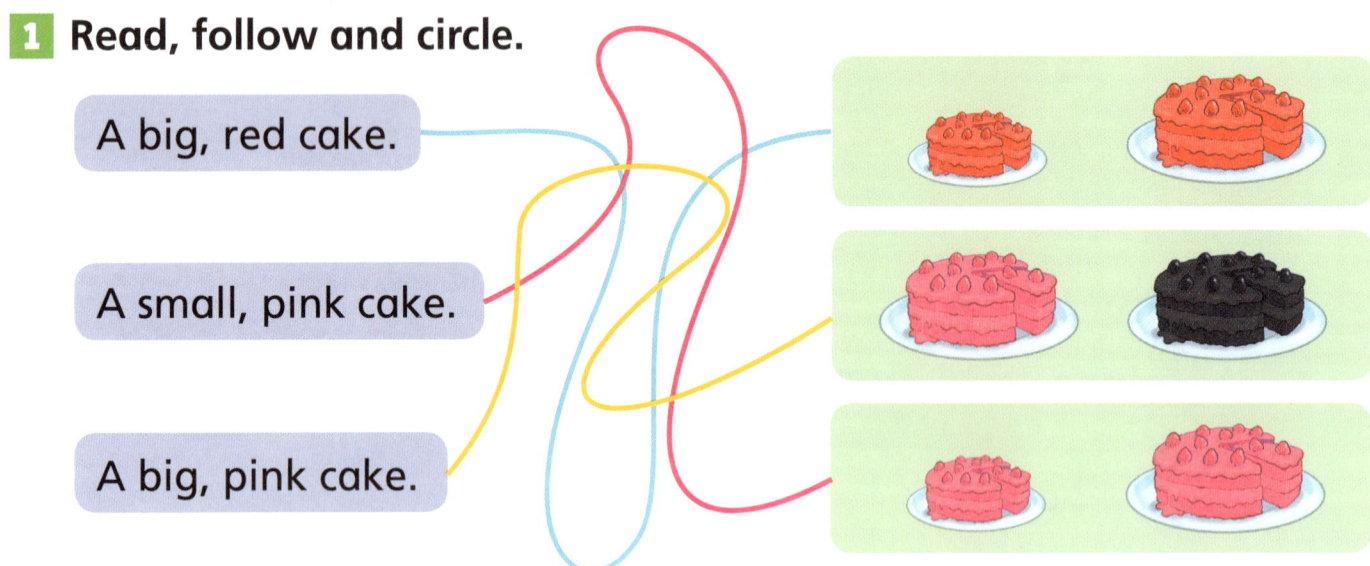

Grandpa's idea

My idea

Let's make a cake!

A cake comes out.

It's _____.

I'm hungry.

Let's make a new cake!

A cake comes out.

It's _____.

I'm _____.

Book Club Extra
Write about the characters on page 6. Use *in front of / behind / next to*.

Lesson 8 Communication 3

1 Listen and tick ✔. Listen and chant. 🔊73

2 💬 Communicate Play the ask and answer game with your friends.

Start

How to play
Play in teams of 2.
Move your counter. Ask and answer.
Correct question = 1 point
Correct answer = 1 point. **10 points wins!**

You need:

Can you see a lake?

Pronunciation today / lake

33

3 Lesson 9 Round Up

1 Look, circle and write.

 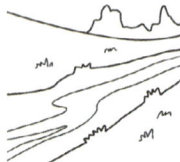

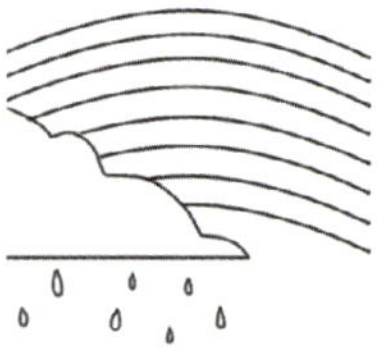

d	e	e	r	r	s	f
l	o	r	n	a	c	o
f	w	i	h	i	a	x
a	l	v	t	n	m	v
r	h	e	m	b	t	d
m	p	r	r	o	r	e
t	e	t	t	w	e	o
f	s	p	i	d	e	r

1 _____ 2 _____

3 _____ 4 _____

5 _____ 6 _____

7 _____ 8 _____

2 Write the words in the correct order. Write the animals.

next   It's   to   tree.   the

1 *It's next to the tree.*

front   of   It's   in   the   tree.

2 _____

behind   It's   tree.   the

3 _____

1 *fox*   2 _____   3 _____

Finished?
Draw and write your favourite words in Unit 3.

Lesson 1 Vocabulary

4 At the station

1 Write. Draw an arrow ➔ for each picture.

e e e e e e e e

~~a~~ a a a a a

~~o~~ o o o o

~~i~~ i i i

1 sh o rt h a i r

2 l__ng h____r

3 br__wn __y__s

4 d__rk h____r

5 fr__ckl__s

6 bl__nd h____r

7 __y__br__ws

8 gl__ss__s

Finished?
What do you look like? Write. *I've got …*

35

4 Lesson 2 Grammar

1 Read and circle.

He's got short / long hair.
He's got glasses / freckles.

She's got dark / blond hair.
She's got brown / blue eyes.

He's got freckles / glasses.
He's got brown / blue eyes.

She's got dark / blond hair.
She's got long / short hair.

2 Be creative Draw 2 people you know. Write.

He's got _____

_____.

She's got _____

_____.

Finished?
Write 2 sentences about your mum or dad.

Lesson 3 Culture **4**

1 Read and tick ✓ or cross ✗.

This is a bus driver.

She's got long hair. ☐

She's got blond hair. ☐

This is a postman.

He's got short hair. ☐

He's got big eyebrows. ☐

This is a police officer.

He's got blond hair. ☐

He's got glasses. ☐

2 Be creative **Who do you see in town? Draw and write.**

He's / She's got

_____

_____

_____.

4 Lesson 4 Everyday language and Values

1 💭 Think Circle the children being polite.

2 Read, find and circle.

Our Values
Are you polite to adults?

He's got short hair.
(Yes) / No

She's got dark hair.
Yes / No

He's got glasses.
Yes / No

She's got freckles.
Yes / No

3 💬 Communicate Write. Act out at home.

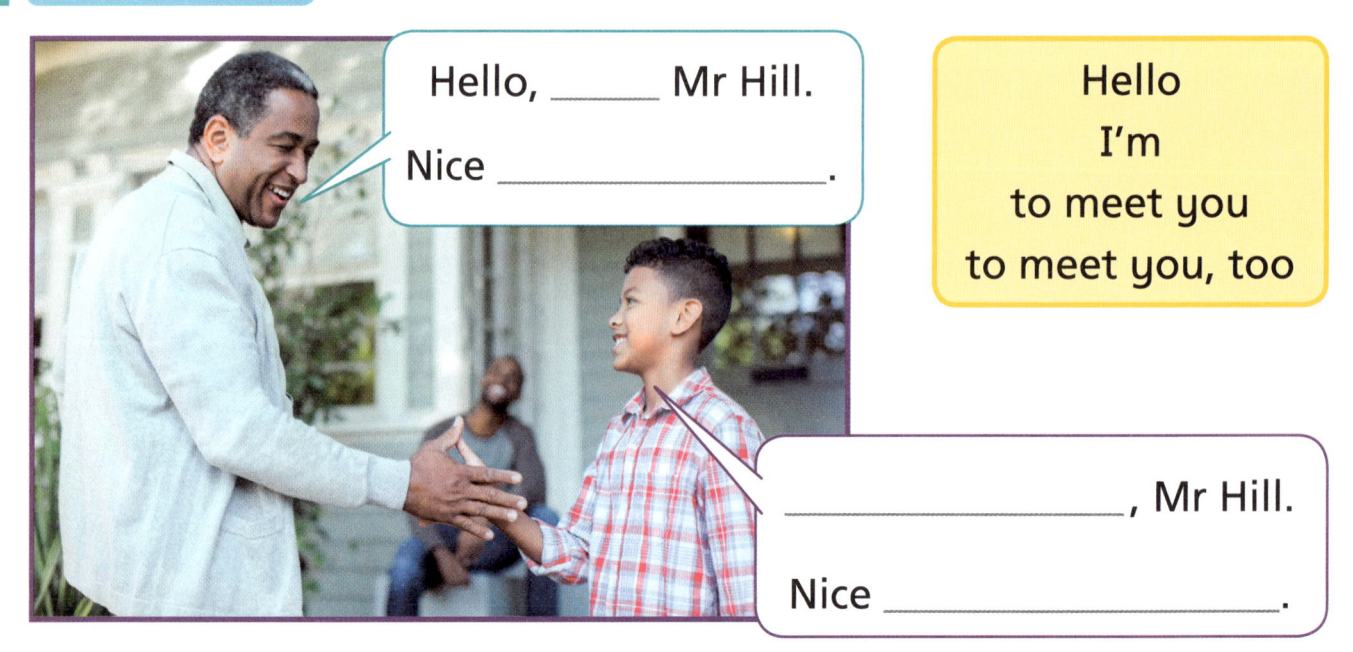

Hello, _____ Mr Hill.

Nice _____.

Hello
I'm
to meet you
to meet you, too

_____, Mr Hill.

Nice _____.

38

Uncle Brian's visit

Lesson 5 Story **4**

1 🍀 **Think** Remember the story. Number the pictures in order.

2 Write. glasses   long   freckles

1. He's got _____ hair.
2. He's got _____.
3. He's got _____.

3 💡 **Be creative** Draw Uncle Brian. Write.

Uncle Brian has got _____ hair.

He's got _____.

He's got _____.

Finished?
Write a description of Anna, Oscar or Dad.

4 Lesson 6 Vocabulary and Grammar

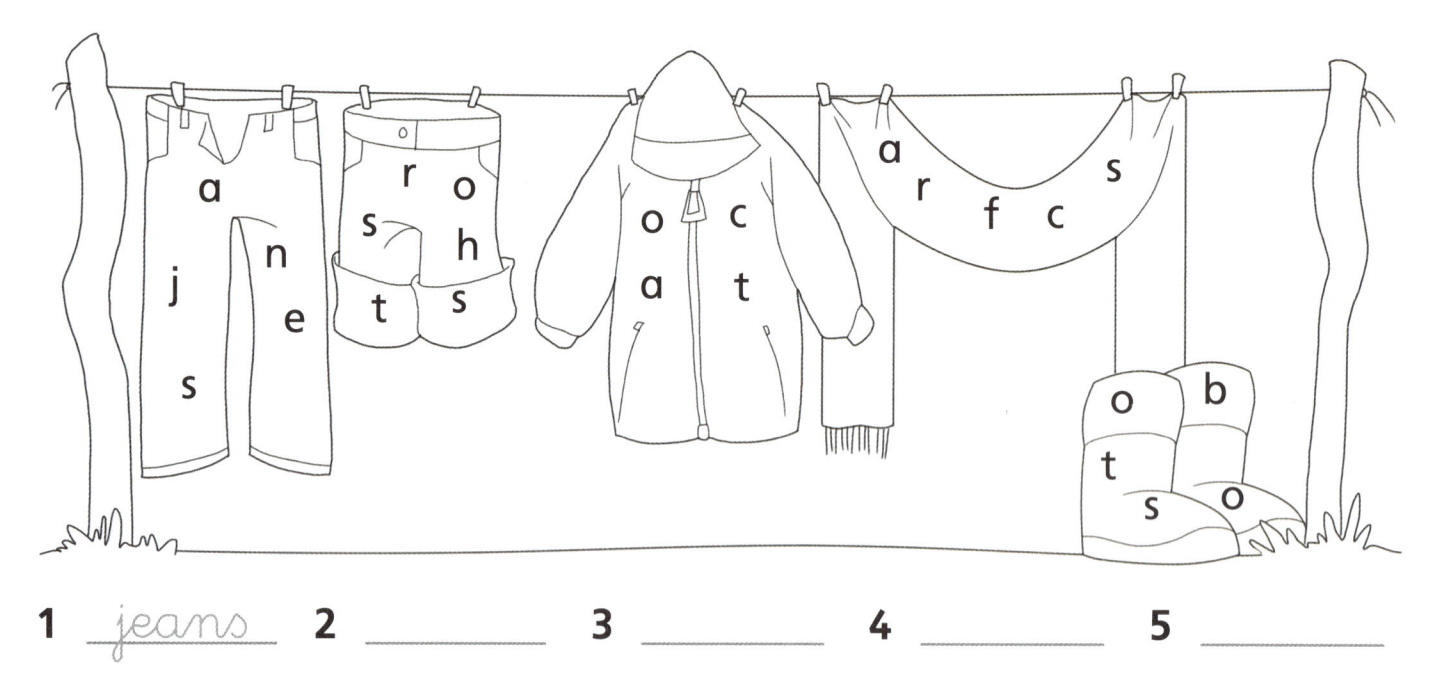

1 Look and write.

1 _jeans_ 2 _____ 3 _____ 4 _____ 5 _____

2 Read and colour. Look and write.

He's wearing a yellow T-shirt.
He's wearing blue shorts.
He's wearing green boots.

She's wearing _____.
_____
_____

Finished?
What are you wearing? Write *I'm wearing ...*

Rooftops Book Club

Lesson 7 Literacy **4**

1 Look and write.

> hit   eat   count   look for   ask

1 _____   2 _____   3 _____   4 _____   5 _____

2 Read and mime or do.

A
Ask your friend's name.
Count the desks in the class.
Eat a sandwich!
Hit your desk.
Look for a red pen.

B
Ask your friend's age.
Count the chairs in the class.
Eat a banana!
Hit your chair.
Look for a blue pencil.

3 Read and write *Yes* or *No*.

1 Grandpa counts 3, 2, 1. _____
2 Grandpa hits the machine. _____
3 A small, black cake comes out. _____
4 Clunk can see the cake. _____ 
5 The cake is pink. _____
6 Mum is happy. _____

Book Club Extra
Write a description of Rosie or Ben.

4 Lesson 8 Communication

1 Listen and tick ✓. Listen and chant. 🔊 93

2 💬 Communicate Play the superhero game. Tick ✓ and draw. Describe and draw.

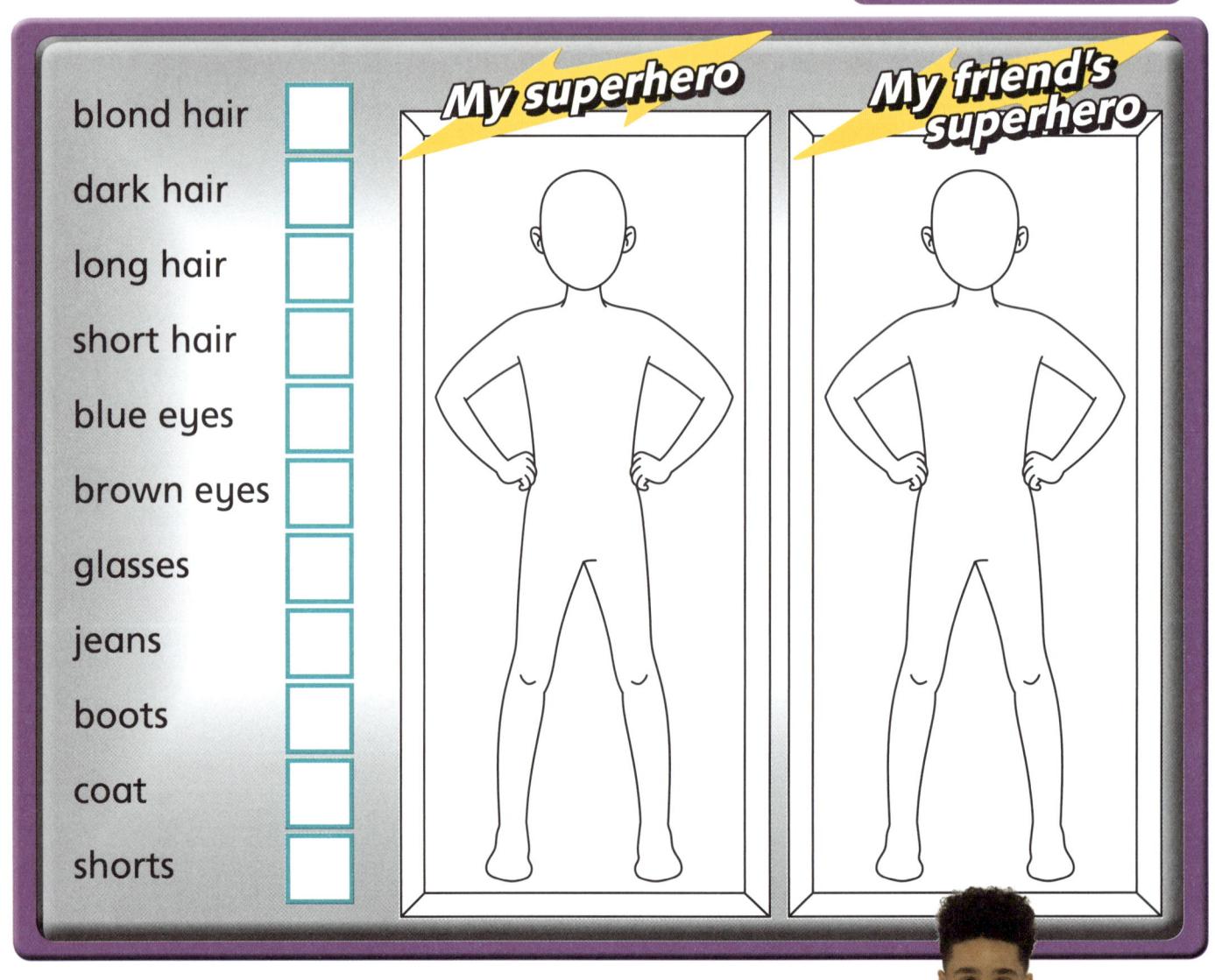

You need: ✏️

- blond hair ☐
- dark hair ☐
- long hair ☐
- short hair ☐
- blue eyes ☐
- brown eyes ☐
- glasses ☐
- jeans ☐
- boots ☐
- coat ☐
- shorts ☐

My superhero

My friend's superhero

She's got dark hair and glasses.

42 | **Pronunciation** park / glasses

Lesson 9 Round Up **4**

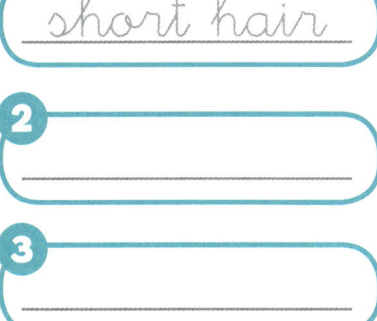

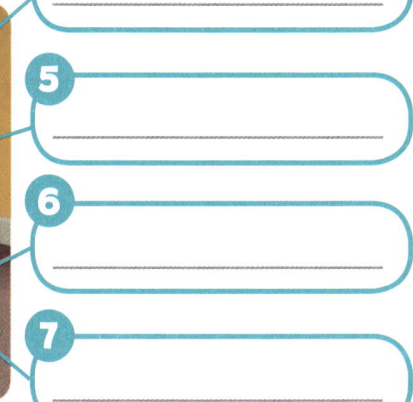

1 Write.

1. short hair
2. _____
3. _____ 
4. _____
5. _____
6. _____
7. _____

2 Read and write. Colour the clothes.

> yellow boots   a green scarf   long hair   short hair
> freckles   glasses   a red coat   pink shorts

1. 
She's got _____.
She's wearing _____.

2. 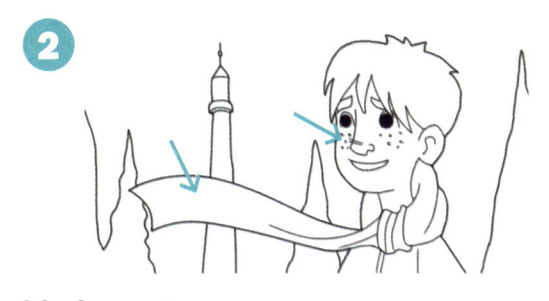
He's got _____.
He's wearing _____.

3. 
He's got _____.
He's wearing _____.

4.
_____
_____

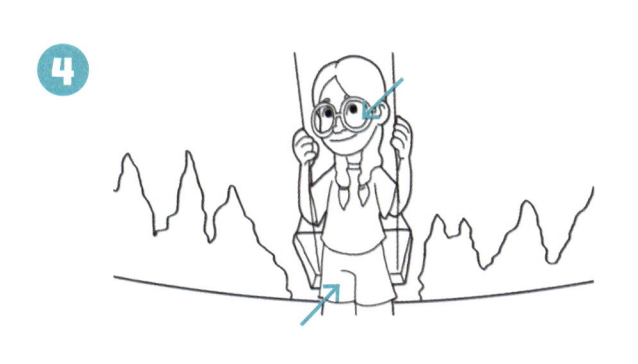

Finished?
Draw and write your favourite words in Unit 4.

Rooftops Review

1 💬 **Communicate** Find and circle. Say more countryside words you can see.

- a rainbow
- a fox
- a farm
- a spider
- She's wearing shorts.
- a tree
- He's got glasses.
- He's wearing a coat.
- She's got blond hair.

Finished?
Find and follow the footprints. Write *Where's the deer / hedgehog / owl? It's …*

Review 2

2 🗨 Think   Read and write more words.

Clothes and faces	4 legs	Town and country
coat	rabbit	hill

3 Join the dots and draw. Read and write.

1

Can you see an animal?

_____

It's a _____.

It's in front of the

_____.

2

Can you see a boy?

_____

She's a girl. _____ got freckles

and _____. She's _____

boots and _____.

Finished?
What else can you see in the picture on page 44? Write.

45

Lesson 1 Vocabulary

5 At the farm

1 Write and draw.

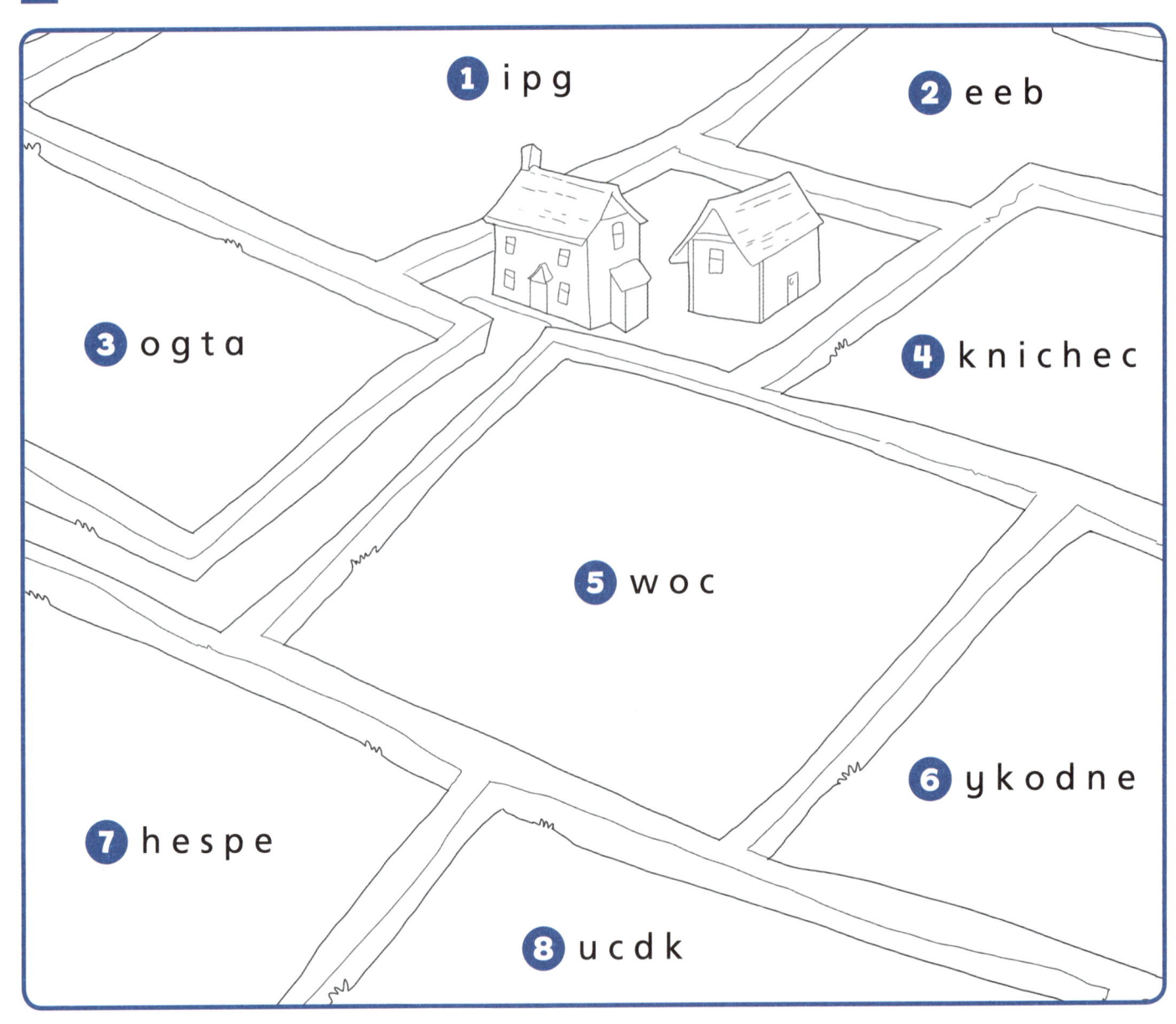

1. i p g
2. e e b
3. o g t a
4. k n i c h e c
5. w o c
6. y k o d n e
7. h e s p e
8. u c d k

1 _____ 2 _____ 3 _____ 4 _____
5 _____ 6 _____ 7 _____ 8 _____

Finished?
Draw a tree, a rainbow, … . Write *I can see …*

46

Lesson 2 Grammar **5**

1 **Read and tick ✓ Yes or No.**

	Yes	No			Yes	No
1 There's a donkey.	☐	☐	5 There are 6 cows.		☐	☐
2 There are 5 goats.	☐	☐	6 There are 5 bees.		☐	☐
3 There are 4 ducks.	☐	☐	7 There are 2 pigs.		☐	☐
4 There are 8 chickens.	☐	☐	8 There's a sheep.		☐	☐

2 **Circle, count and write.**

1 (cow)   *There are 7 cows.*

2 (goat)   _____

3 (pig)   _____

4 (chicken) _____

Finished?
Finished? Write about things in your classroom. *There are (20 desks).*

47

5
Lesson 3 Culture

1 Listen and circle the correct words. 🔊 103

2 Look, read and number.

1.
There are 3 **sisters** / **brothers**.
There's a **donkey** / **horse**.

2.
There's a **dog** / **cat**.
There are 2 **brothers** / **sisters**.

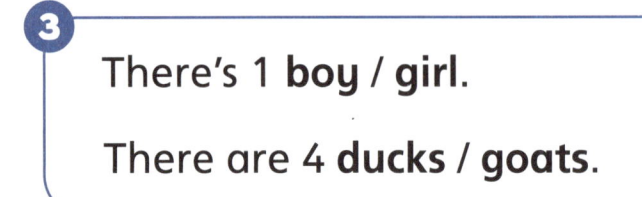

3.
There's 1 **boy** / **girl**.
There are 4 **ducks** / **goats**.

3 Be creative Imagine a farm near you. Draw and write.

Come to the farm!

There's a _____.

There are _____.

You can _____.

Lesson 4 Everyday language and Values 5

1 💭 Think Look and tick ✓ the children following the country code.

Our Values
Do you follow the country code?

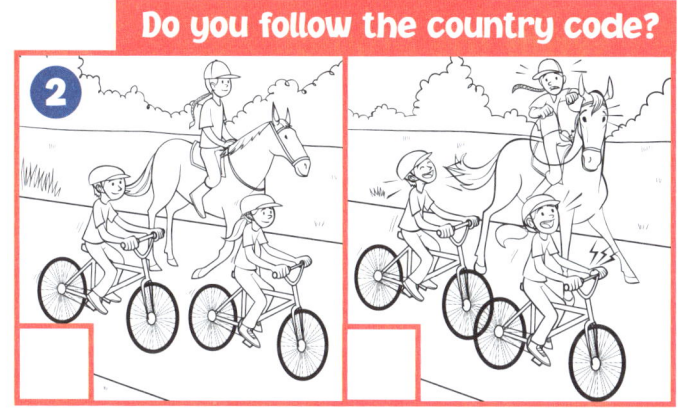

2 Look again. Read and number.

Don't touch!  | Please close the gate  | Don't shout!  | Don't run after the animals

3 💬 Communicate Write. Act out with your family.

you   How many
2   please

_____ tickets?

_____ tickets, _____.

Thank _____.

5 Lesson 5 Story

The mysterious animal

1 💭 **Think** Remember the story. Match.

2 Write the animal.

1.   2.   3.

d___k__y   m_____   c_____

3 💡 **Be creative** Draw the animal Neena finds. Write.

It's an _____.

It's in the _____.

Finished?
Draw and write the animals from the story. *There's a pig …*

Lesson 6 Vocabulary and Grammar

1 What's missing? Write.
2 Draw.

ears   teeth   ~~feathers~~   wings   feet

1 It hasn't got _feathers_.

2 It hasn't got _____.

3 It hasn't got _____.

4 It hasn't got _____.

5 It hasn't got _____.

3 Read and tick ✓. Write and draw.

This is my favourite animal.

It's got 4 big feet.

It's got big ears.

It hasn't got wings.

It hasn't got feathers.

It's got big teeth.

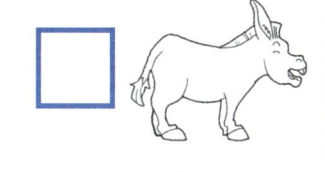

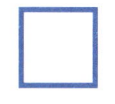

☐   ☐
☐    ☐

This is my favourite animal.

It's got _____.

_____.

_____.

_____.

_____.

Finished?
Write about 1 of the other animals in Activity 3.

51

Lesson 7 Literacy

Rooftops Book Club

1 Read and write. like   kitchen   ice cream   café   red

I'm in the _____.

There's a big _____, strawberry _____ cake!

I'm in the _____.
I _____ this cake!

2 What happens next? Choose an idea. Draw and write.

Ideas

Grandpa has got a new machine. It makes …

Grandpa puts … in the cake machine. It makes a …

Rosie and Ben have got a present for Grandpa. It's a …

Clunk makes a cake. It's …

The next day …
_____
_____

Book Club Extra
Count the cakes in the café on page 12. Write *There are …*

Lesson 8 Communication   5

1 Listen and tick ✓. Listen and chant. 🔊 114

2 💬 Communicate   Play the farm game. Complete the sentences to win.

1 There's a _____.

   It's got _____.

2 There's a _____.

   It's got _____.

3 There are _____.

4 There are _____.

You need:

There are 4 cows.

Pronunciation girl / purple   53

5 Lesson 9 Round Up

1 Look, circle and write.

1. _____ 
2. _____ 
3. _____ 
4. _____

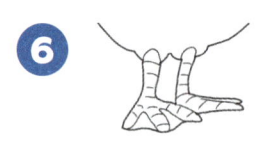

f	d	o	n	k	e	y	e
v	g	o	a	t	s	n	s
a	n	z	l	q	h	w	i
c	h	i	c	k	e	n	j
f	e	a	t	h	e	r	s
w	i	n	g	s	p	k	t
q	t	f	e	e	t	y	j
e	a	f	b	e	e	i	p

5. _____
6. _____
7. _____
8. _____

2 Read and write. Choose and write.

It's got feathers.   It's got _____.

It's got big ears.   It's _____.

It hasn't got teeth.   It hasn't got _____.

It's an _____.   It's a _____.

3 Look, count and write. Say.

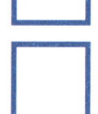

1 cow
☐ _____
☐ _____
☐ _____

Finished?
Draw and write your favourite words in Unit 5.

Lesson 1 Vocabulary

6 At the fair

1 Write. **2** Draw and colour.

1 _____ (popcorn)
2 _____ (juice)
3 _____ (milk)
4 _____ (lemonade)
5 _____ (soup)
6 _____ (pizza)
7 _____ (salad)
8 _____ (pasta)

Finished?
Write words you know in 2 lists: food / drinks.

6 Lesson 2 Grammar

1 **Read and number.**

What are you eating? I'm eating salad.

What are you drinking? I'm drinking lemonade.

What are you drinking? I'm drinking milk.

What are you eating? I'm eating soup.

2 **Write.**   **3** **Follow and write.**

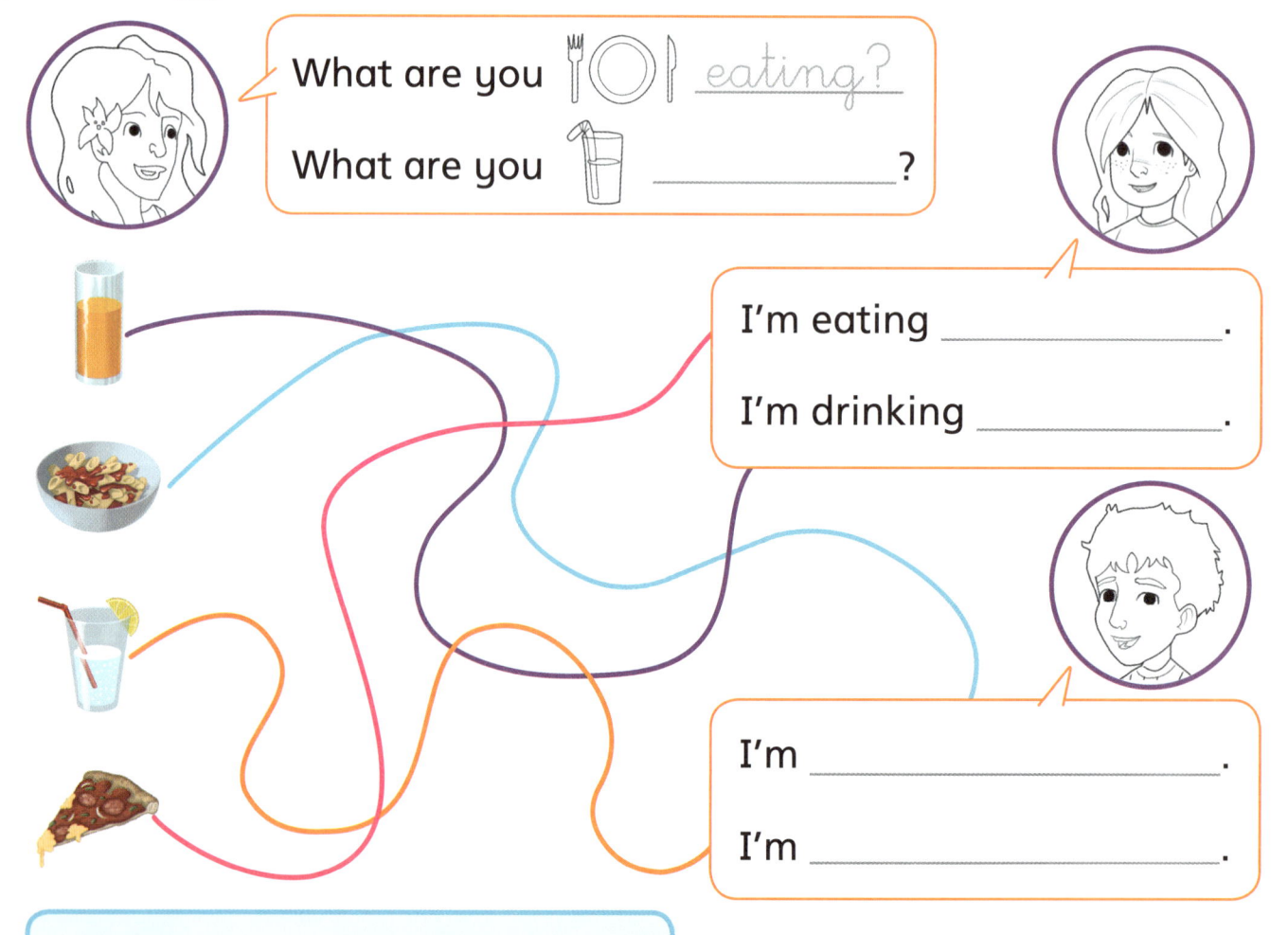

What are you eating?

What are you _____?

I'm eating _____.

I'm drinking _____.

I'm _____.

I'm _____.

Finished?
Choose 2 foods. Draw and write *I like* …

Lesson 3 Culture **6**

1 **Read and number.**

1 I'm at the fair. Come on! Let's play a game! Look! There are some ducks on the water.

2 Mmm. I'm hungry. I like pizza.

3 I'm wearing a red dress and a white hat. I can dance!

2 **Be creative** Imagine a fair near you. Draw and write.

I can see _____.

I like _____.

I'm wearing _____.

I'm eating _____.

6 Lesson 4 Everyday language and Values

Our Values — Do you recycle?

1 💭 **Think** Circle 4 children who are recycling.

"I'd like some lemonade, please."

2 What do you recycle? Look and tick ✓.

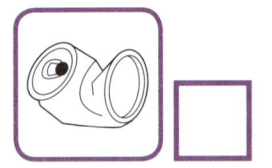

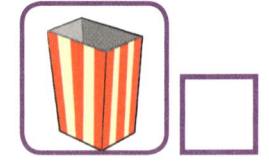

3 💬 **Communicate** Look, write and act out at home.

4 What can you recycle? Ask your family and tick ✓.

"I'd like some _____, please."

"Here you are."

Do you recycle?

Lesson 5 Story **6**

Are you ready?

1 🗨 **Think** Remember the story. Match. Write.

old T-shirt

green dress

big coat

white cap

Anna is wearing a _____.   Oscar is wearing a _____.

Neena is wearing a _____.   TJ is wearing an _____.

2 💡 **Be creative** What's missing? Draw.

3 What does Nizzy like? Draw ☺ or ☹.

Finished?
Look again and draw ☺ or ☹ for you. Draw yourself in the show.

59

6 Lesson 6 Vocabulary and Grammar

1 Look and write.

> dressing up   painting   ~~acting~~
> playing music   making posters

acting

2 Look and write.

1. I don't like _____.

2. I like _____.

3. _____

4. _____

Finished?
Write for you: *I like … I don't like …*

Lesson 7 Literacy **6**

Rooftops Book Club

1 Look and write. Write the secret word.

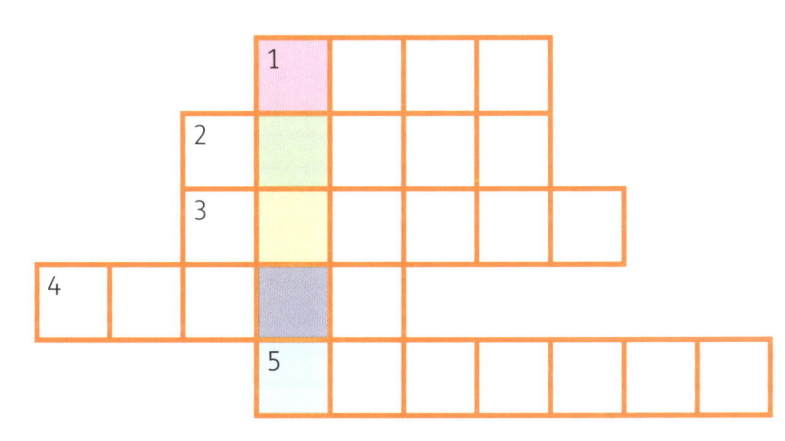

The secret word is: ☐☐☐☐☐

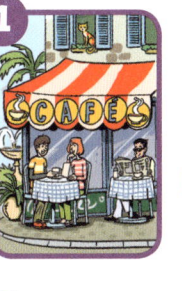

2 Complete the story summary.

> eggs   pink   café   machine   sugar   black

Grandpa has got a new _____.

He puts _____, flour and butter in the machine.

Clunks puts in _____ and strawberries.

A cake comes out.

It's small and _____.

Grandpa makes a new cake.

It's _____.

Rosie and Ben go to the _____.

Book Club Extra
Write. *My favourite character / page / picture is …*

6 Lesson 8 Communication

1 Listen and tick ✓. Listen and chant. 🔊 133

2 💬 Communicate Draw. Play bingo with your friends.

popcorn

dressing up

pizza

playing music

soup

acting

Bingo!

62 Pronunciation three / teeth

Lesson 9 Round Up 6

1 Look and write.

1 p_ainting_
2 p_____n
3 m___k
4 p_____g m____c

5 l_____e
6 p___t_
7 s____d
8 d_____g __p

2 Look again and write.

1 I like painting.

2 I'm _____.

3 I'm _____.

4 I _____.

Finished?
Draw and write your favourite words in Unit 6.

63

Rooftops Review

1 💬 **Communicate**   Find and count. Write the number. Tell your friend.

- 🐄 cows ☐
- 🐑 sheep ☐
- 🪰 wings ☐
- 🎻 playing music ☐
- 🥤 drinking juice ☐
- 🍿 eating popcorn ☐
- 🐴 donkeys ☐
- 🐝 bees ☐
- 🍕 eating pizza ☐

Finished? Look and find TJ! What's he doing? Write.

Review 3

2 🧠 Think Read and write more words.

Wings
owl

Drinks
juice

Foods with a 'p'
peaches

3 Read and tick ✓. Draw your costume. Write.

Look! I'm a chicken!
I've got brown wings. I've got a tail.
I've got big feathers and yellow feet.
I'm drinking lemonade.
I'm eating popcorn.
I like dressing up!

Look! I'm a _____.

I've got _____.

I've got _____.

I'm drinking _____

and I'm _____.

Finished?
Draw an animal and label all the parts you know.

Happy Halloween

1 Read and match.

1 troll
2 skeleton
3 cobwebs
4 wizard
5 fairy
6 spider

2 Look and write. Tick ✓ your favourite costume.

troll   wizard   spider   fairy   skeleton   cobwebs

1 He's a _____.
2 He's a _____.
3 She's a _____.
4 She's a _____.
5 He's a _____.
6 She's got _____.

Finished?
Draw a Halloween costume for you.

Merry Christmas

1 Read and number.

1 ~~Father Christmas~~   2 reindeer   3 bells
4 chimney   5 lights   6 snowman

2 What's missing? Look again. Draw and write.

1. I've got 5 *lights* .

2. I've got a _____ .

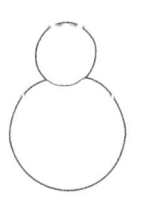

3. I've got 2 _____ .

4. This is a _____ .

5. This is _____ .

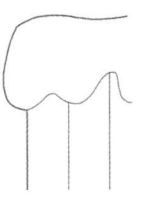

6. This is _____ .

Finished?
Draw a gingerbread house.

67

Happy Easter

1 Look, read and write.

2 Listen and check. 🔊 143

spice   flour   sugar   milk   Butter
Hot cross buns   raisins

Hot cross buns! _____ ! Hot cross buns!

Let's make yummy hot cross buns!

_____, sugar, _____ and _____.

Mix and bake for half an hour!

_____! Hot cross buns!

Let's make yummy hot cross buns!

Butter, _____, _____, _____,

Hot cross buns are very nice!

3 Where's the hot cross bun? Read and draw.

① 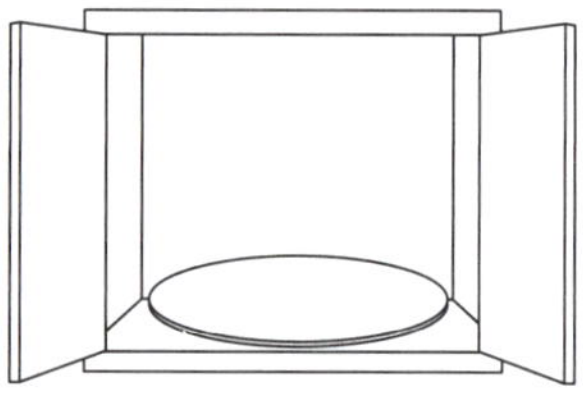 It's in the cupboard.

② 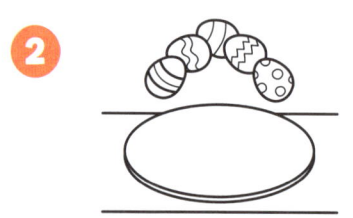 It's under the eggs.

③ 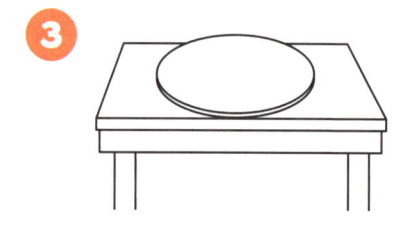 It's on the table.

④  It's next to the raisins.

⑤  It's in front of the flour.

⑥  It's behind the flowers.

Finished? Draw an Easter egg.

68

6 Food at the fair

This book belongs to

Class _____

He's eating salad.

4

He's drinking juice.

5

6 Make your mini-book.

69

7

I'm drinking _____ .

2

I'm at the fair. I'm eating pasta. Pasta is my favourite food!

6

I'm eating _____ .

3

He's drinking lemonade.

70

5 A farm visit

This book belongs to

Class _____

There are 5 chickens.

4

There's a cow.

5

5 Make your mini-book.

7

There are _____.

6 There's a _____.

2 It's fun on the farm!
There's a sheep.

3 There's a goat.

72

4 A museum in my town

This book belongs to

Class

Look at the train!
This train is old.

4

This is the train driver.
He's got short hair.

5

4 Make your mini-book.

7

This is a museum I like.
I'm at the _____.

2

Look at me!
I've got freckles.

6

This is me.
I've got _____.

3

My dad has got glasses.

74

3 Let's explore!

This book belongs to

Class

4 Look! I can see a farm.

This is a hill. 5

3 Make your mini-book.

7

My favourite place is the _____.

2

Let's visit our region.
Can you see the river?

6 This is where I live.

3 This is a road.

2 Playtime

This book belongs to

Class

Let's skip!
He can jump.

4

Let's play tag!
He can run.

5

---

2 Make your mini-book.

7

I can _____.

2

I'm in the playground.
I can draw. I can write.

3

She can hop.

6

This is my school.
Let's play a game!

1 At home

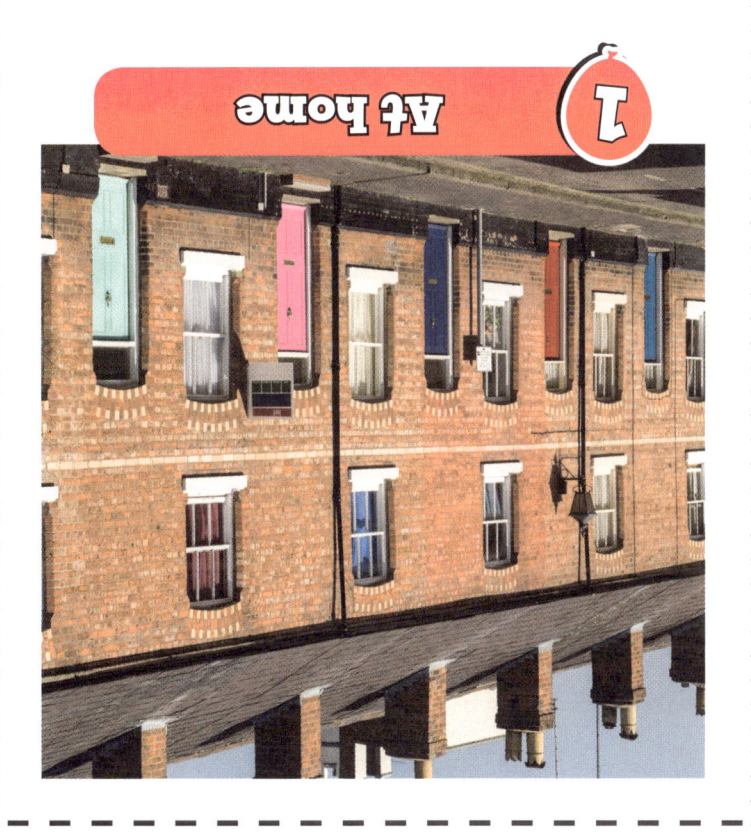

This book belongs to _____

Class _____

4 This is my sister.
She's in the living room.

5 Now she's in the garden.

1 Make your mini-book.

7

I'm in the _____.

2

This is my home.
I'm in my bedroom.

6

This is my home.

3

This is my dad.
He's in the kitchen.